HADES
SPEAKS!

SECRETS OF THE ANCIENT GODS

HADES SPEAKS!

A GUIDE TO THE UNDERWORLD BY THE GREEK GOD OF THE DEAD

VICKY ALVEAR SHECTER
ILLUSTRATIONS BY J. E. LARSON

BOYDS MILLS PRESS
AN IMPRINT OF HIGHLIGHTS
Honesdale, Pennsylvania

The author wishes to thank Dr. Jasper Gaunt, curator of the Greek and Roman Galleries at the Michael C. Carlos Museum of Antiquities at Emory University, and Christina Marinelli, M.A., for their valuable assistance in the preparation of this book.

Boyds Mills Press, Inc.
An Imprint of Highlights
815 Church Street
Honesdale, Pennsylvania 18431
Printed in the United States of America
ISBN: 978-1-62091-598-1
Library of Congress Control Number: 2014933622
First edition
10 9 8 7 6 5 4 3 2 1
The text of this book is set in Century Schoolbook
and Gill Sans STD.
The illustrations are done in pen and ink.

For Matthew and Aliya
—VAS

To Yvy, who can mend spirits
—JEL

CONTENTS

CAUTION

HADES, THE ANCIENT GREEK GOD of the Dead, wants you to know that the stories included in this book represent the works of many Greek and Roman writers and poets over hundreds and hundreds of years. Beliefs about the Greek and Roman afterworld changed by era, location, poet, and philosopher. Hades chose the details that he thought best captured the essence of ancient Greek and Roman beliefs about the afterlife—and also the ones that had the highest chance of creeping you out.

GREETINGS, MORTAL!

ALLOW ME TO INTRODUCE MYSELF. I am Hades, king of the ancient Greek underworld, also known as "The God of the Dead," "The Dark Lord," and "Lord of the Place of Darkness." The Romans also called me Pluto, which meant "wealth." And not just because I was "rich" in good looks and charm, but because I had control of all the gold and silver under the earth.

Both the Greeks and the Romans sometimes referred to me as "He Who Must Not Be Named." Yes, that's right. Way before Voldemort and Harry Potter, the ancients were afraid to call my name out loud. They feared that if I heard them, I'd be compelled to drag them down to the underworld.

Honestly, I found this idea quite insulting. I was a *king*. A ruler. I did not bag and tag humans like some evil hunter whenever I heard my name. I let my monstrous minions do that.

You will meet many of them on this tour of my home—monsters such as the multi-headed dog Cerberus and the goat-legged, flame-haired vampire demon Empusa, among many others.

But do not be afraid. They will not touch you, as long as you stay near me. Oh, also, do not eat any of the luscious pomegranates that grow near my palace, because if you do, you will never return to the land of the living. Why rush things, right?

Please, step right up onto my gleaming chariot, led by four giant dark horses. Hold on tight, because when my stallions start racing, we run straight down into a hole in the ground. The noise of the earth opening is spectacular, by the way—kind of like the worst tearing, ripping, crashing sound you can imagine.

What? You'd rather not "fly" into the ground at top speed with me on my chariot? Fine, we'll go the boring way. We'll walk down through one of my many secret cave entrances. (There's one right outside your bedroom.)

Are you ready? I've been waiting for you to visit me for a very long time. . . .

DOWN, DOWN, DOWN ...

I HOPE YOU'RE NOT AFRAID of the dark. If you are, you might consider shutting this book and running outside to play with bubbles in the sunshine. Seriously, my world is the complete absence of light—dark, dim, gloomy, sinister, you name it. No birds chirping in the sunlight around here. Instead, you might find some bloodthirsty bats and even an occasional winged Fury screeching at us.

If you think you can handle it, follow me into this cave entrance. Ahhhh—cold, musty, moldy, wet darkness. The blackness embraces you like a thick cloak of slime, doesn't it?

I hope you're wearing comfortable shoes, too. It's a

long way down. My people—the ancient Greeks—were a strong, hardy lot and would not have been fazed by this long descent into darkness.

The ancient Greeks lived more than 2,500 years ago and were responsible for many of the things you take for granted today, such as democracy, freedom of speech, theater, money, the Olympic Games, and crazy politicians.

In fact, Greece is often called the "cradle of Western civilization." In other words, without us, "you" wouldn't be you. You may thank us for this gift later—preferably with a sacrifice of gold. In my name, if you please.

Anyway, so impressive were my people, the Romans copied just about everything they could steal—er, I mean "borrow"—from us, including Greek architecture, art, philosophy, sculpture, theater, and most importantly, us Greek gods. The Romans renamed us, of course, but we'll talk about those toga-wearing thieves later.

My people lived on mainland Greece and its surrounding islands. Most of Greece is a rocky, mountainous place, which created tough, rugged, adventuresome people. The Greeks sailed into regions unknown (to them, anyway) and established cities in what is now Turkey and even Italy.

While the ancient Greeks were brilliant, they were also a tad warlike. They battled among their many city-states like you and your friends fight for the last piece of candy in the bowl. Athens fought Sparta in a war that lasted decades and got just about every city-state involved in picking sides.

They also fought off invasions from their dreaded enemies, the Persians. But don't get me wrong. I'm not complaining about all that death and destruction. It made my underworld a very busy place.

Aside from their many innovations, however, it is my opinion that the Greek's greatest achievement was—and I say this with all humility—the creation of us, the Greek gods.

HOW IT ALL STARTED

The Greeks believed that gods of earth (Gaia) and sky (Ouranos) gave birth to the first gods of the world, the Titans. Kronos, the Titan god of time and age, overthrew his father and took control of the cosmos. His angry parents foretold that one of Kronos's own children would depose him, which is why we gods began as baby food.

Kronos's brilliant plan for getting around the prophecy was to eat his kids as soon as his wife Rhea bore them. See, because we were immortal, he couldn't actually *kill* us. But he could keep us prisoners inside himself. He started by gobbling my sisters—Hestia, Demeter, and Hera. I came next—making me the firstborn son, I should point out—followed by Poseidon.

Our mom, Rhea, was not happy about her husband's baby-eating habit, but she didn't know how to stop him.

Finally, by the time my *little* brother Zeus was born, she came up with a plan. (Really, Mom? Nothing occurred to you until the sixth child?)

Rhea gave birth to Zeus in secret, sent him to a faraway cave, and gave Kronos a rock wrapped in a baby blanket to eat instead. Our father swallowed the rock and Zeus got to grow up with beautiful nymph nannies and dancing warriors for entertainment and protection. Talk about spoiled! Meanwhile, the rest us spent our time chillin' in the belly of the beast.

Finally, when Zeus grew up, he made Kronos vomit us out (*ewwww*, I know).Together, my siblings and I defeated dear ol' dad and the other Titans, hurling them deep into the belly of the earth, the lowest level of Tartaros. I call it the pit of punishment.

WHEN WINNING MEANT LOSING

We won the world! But then we had to figure out how to manage it. As the eldest son, I demanded the lion's share. But baby brother Zeus disagreed. Yeah, he rescued us, and I guess we all owed him one, but still.

We compromised and decided to draw lots. And surprise, surprise—baby brother ended up with all the best bits. Zeus got the earth, the sky, thunder, justice, and all the nations. Poseidon got all the seas and fresh waters, horses, and earthquakes. And me—what did I get?

The dead and the dark, dismal underworld. Seriously?

I am convinced my little brother rigged the lottery. He claims that I'm just jealous, but he is completely and utterly wrong. Jealousy is beneath me.

Still, it irks me that you know so little about me, yet you know so much about my *younger* brothers. I bet it's hard for many of you to even conjure up an *image* of me. And why is that? Because statues and paintings of my brothers and sisters were *everywhere* in ancient Greece. But there were hardly any of me. This is an outrage that has bothered me for more than a millennium.

My people built temples to my brothers, Zeus and Poseidon. They built temples to Athena, Artemis, Aphrodite, and many other godlings (minor gods). They even built temples and cult centers devoted to demigod heroes such as Herakles (you know him by his Roman name, Hercules). But they hardly had *any* temples or cult centers devoted to *me*.

Excuse me, but how could there be more shrines devoted to a muscular meathead—Herakles—than temples devoted to the one god they'd hang out with for *eternity*? It wasn't right!

Herakles, by the way, is like homework—useless, boring, and stupid. Yet you will meet him down here many times for the simple reason that I cannot get rid of that club-carrying, lion cloak–wearing muscle man to save my life. He sneaks down here so often that he's become a real pain in the backside. And I mean that literally, as you will see in chapter four.

Also, that scrappy son of Zeus once actually *shot* me in the shoulder with an arrow, right outside my gates. I had to go all the way to Mount Olympus to be treated by the physician to the gods, Paeeon (*pea*-en). Zeus and his out-of-control kids will be the death of me, I swear.

Zeus himself is no saint either, by the way. Not only did he take most of the "good stuff" on the planet, he's constantly meddling in my world. Let me give you an example. Originally, the Olympic Games honored the *dead*. That's right; they started out as funerary contests. The games were designed to appease me by honoring the recently fallen, especially during a war.

Somehow, over the ages, the Olympic Games turned into a massive festival to honor Zeus! Now, no one remembers that they originally began as a way to honor the dead, which means honoring the *king* of the dead—*me*.

Zeus is the little brother from hell, you guys. Seriously.

HOMER'S BLIND SPOT

The most famous Greek poet, Homer (no, not the cartoon character Homer Simpson—crack open a book, kid!) wrote that my realm was at the "end" of the earth on the western shore of the "river" Oceanus. He also said it was beyond the gates of the sun and the land of dreams.

Could he have been *any* more vague? That unseeing bard had a blind spot about my world. Just sayin'.

Eventually, almost all ancient Greeks and Romans came to believe that my realm was underground and that it was dark, dank, miserable, and smelly. Now, I ask you, does it stink down here? (Be careful how you answer, kid.) One Greek playwright even described my realm as a "mass of mire" filled with "everlasting dung."

Really? Every poop in the history of the world ends up in "my" house?

I ask you—where's the respect? I mean, this is my *home*, people. How would you like it if I told everyone that your house was filled with poop and stank like rotten eggs, and that no one ever—ever, ever, ever—wanted to come over?

As we get closer to the heart of my world, you might want to memorize the map on the following pages and the path we will take. I highly recommend that you do not get lost. I am not responsible for the actions of my bloodthirsty minions. In case you do get separated from me, go directly to my palace. You'll be safe there. Unless my wife, Persephone (per-*seff*-ah-nee), is in a bad mood, that is.

TITAN'S
PIT

T A R T A R O S

A S P H O D E L
F I E L D S

PHLEGETHON

STYX

COCYTUS

HADES GATES

S T Y X CHARON

O C E A N U S

ODYSSEUS

GROVE OF
PERSEPHONE

WELCOME TO THE LAND OF THE DEAD

EVER NOTICE HOW PEOPLE get my name and my *realm* confused? Yeah, it irritates me, too. My people called my underworld the "House of Hades," which was fine by me. But over time, they shortened it to just "Hades," and you had to figure out if they were referring to my realm or to *me*. Just another example of the disrespect I have suffered for oh-so-long.

As we emerge from the cave tunnel opening, you will notice my wife's small forest in front of us, which my people called the "Grove of Persephone." Follow me through the trails among the skeleton-like black poplars and barren willow trees. I love how the air moving through the dead branches sounds like the moaning of tortured souls. I don't know why people think this is a scary place. Personally, I find these dead trees quite cheerful—the ones that loom over you like monsters about to fall on your head and squish you until you burst like a juicy blister.

That blur of light that just zoomed past us, by the way, is Hermes. I don't like that boy—and not just because he is a son of Zeus. He's the one who brings my wife to the upper world when it's time for her to visit her mom, Demeter (deh-*mee*-ter). Because of that job, Hermes ended up escorting *all* the dead to my realm. Not like they needed an escort, but still. It gave the hyperactive, thieving godling something to do. (Yeah, he's the god of thieves, so *of course* he's Zeus's son.) Plus, having a guide made the Greeks feel like entering my world would be a tad less scary.

As I said, my wife's mother is Demeter, the earth goddess of plants and grain. She is a *Freak. Of. Nature.* And I mean that literally, as you will soon see. Also, she suffers from Possessive Mother Syndrome.

Demeter demands that Persephone live with her for most of the year, leaving me with only three months or so to spend with my wife. During the time that Persephone is with me, Demeter makes the upper world go cold, white, and dead, all because she misses her daughter. She figures, if the queen of nature is going to be sad, then *everybody* needs to suffer, too.

Such a drama queen, am I right?

When Persephone returns to mommy in the spring, Demeter makes everything bloom again in wild exuberance. As if I don't notice the insult *every single year*.

Also, the way she tells it, I "stole" her daughter. In truth, I asked Zeus—Persephone's father—for his daughter's hand in marriage first. He *agreed*. I followed the rules of my people and my era.

What? You say the world has changed so much that women in your time can *choose* their own husbands? And that they can go to school, vote, work, own property, and live independently and freely?

Aw, stop telling crazy stories.

Wait, you're not kidding?

Wow. In ancient Greece, women couldn't do *any* of those things. In fact, women were typically hidden away in the home. Don't tell Persephone about this. She'd likely want to leave for your upper world early, which would cause a warm winter, and then everyone would panic about global warming.

FIENDS ON THE PATH

As we leave my wife's grove, pay no attention to the she-devils coming our way. No, seriously, do *not* make eye contact. You don't want them showing their teeth or claws to you. These scaly, blood-thirsty spirits are Keres (*kur*-ess), the personifications of violent death and death by horrible disease. They tear the souls from the bodies of the fallen on the battlefield and in the sickroom. They are always on the lookout for the dying, so don't lie down anywhere near them, okay?

It suddenly got cooler, didn't it? That means we have now entered the mist of death. It's cold and wet and miserable. But don't worry; the mist won't harm you while you're with me. Seriously, relax, or I'll ask the mist to transform itself into its other form as the dark goddess Achlys (*ack*-liss). A *primordial* being (meaning she was here before any of us), Achlys represents the mist of death that comes over the dying. In her monster form, she is depicted as a pale, emaciated old hag with clacking teeth and stringy hair. She has gross, twisted nails, which she uses to gouge out her cheeks. Blood runs down the sides of her face. It's a good look for her, but I ordered her to show herself to you as a mist today—mostly because I forgot to tell you to bring clean underwear.

THE RIVERS OF MISERY

Smell that brackish water? As we leave the mist of death, we can finally see the five rivers of the underworld. On the right there is Acheron (*ack*-uh-ron), the River of Woe. On the other side is the Cocytus (koh-*kie*-tus), the River of Lamentation. All those cries of misery and pain are like music to my ears.

Around the other side is the Lethe (*lee*-thee), the River of Forgetfulness. One sip, and you lose all memory of your previous life—even your name. Near Tartaros (the pit in the belly of the earth where the

Titans were imprisoned and evil souls are punished) is the Phlegethon (*fleg*-ah-thon), the River of Fire—a special place of torture for evil souls. And finally, there is the Styx, sometimes called the River of Hate.

These rivers separate the upper world from the underworld. So technically, we are not *in* my realm yet—we must cross the Styx first. Fortunately, Charon will ferry us. The ancient Greeks saw the ferryman as a bearded old man with a crooked nose, wearing a conical hat. He was not considered an especially happy guy.

The Etruscans, though—the people who lived in ancient Italy before the Romans—described their underworld ferryman, Charun, as a gruesome brute: blue skin, tusked mouth, and snaky arms. I like our Greek Charon better.

See all those dead wandering aimlessly behind Charon? Those are the ones who forgot to bring a coin for the ferryman. What, you thought Charon worked for *free*? No, he works on a "pay as you go" basis. If you don't pay, you don't go.

The other poor souls wandering behind the ferryman are those who weren't buried at all, which the ancient Greeks and Romans considered a horrible crime.

Skittering among the unburied souls is the monster-goddess Melinoe (mel-*in*-o-ee). Half of her body is pitch-black and the other half is stark white. It's an interesting look. Anyway, she roams around down here on this side of the Styx, gathering the angry

dead—those who were murdered and those who weren't buried. Melinoe leads the angry ghosts on a haunting party in the upper world every night. She loves her job and she's darn good at it.

Melinoe's nightly escorting of the dead to the world of the living was something my people feared very much. They performed a number of rites, or ritual practices, to appease the dead and keep Melinoe's ghosties away.

WARNING: DON'T GET THE RITES WRONG

If you messed up the funerary rites, my people believed that the dead would never leave you in peace. They'd come to you in dreams, send you bad luck, and even appear as ghostly visitations. Worse, they'd haunt your descendants, too. The idea of being harangued by the dead in any shape or form scared my people so much that they came up with a bunch of rules to keep the dead—and me, of course—happy. My people called them funerary rites. I called them entertainment.

They generally included:

STEP 1—THE PROTHESIS (LAYING OUT THE BODY).

The body was bathed and anointed, dressed in a white robe, and laid out on an elevated bed, often with pillows behind the head and shoulders. The feet always faced the door, so that it looked as if the dead person were standing or sitting up to welcome you when you came to pay your respects. This was the time to say your final goodbyes, which involved a lot of wailing, cloth-rending, chest-beating, and hair-pulling. In some eras, the women were also expected to gouge their cheeks with their nails, drawing blood as a sign of their extreme grief.

Bloodied faces, crazy hair, and wild keening—now, that's my kind of party!

The living also worried about being "polluted" or dirtied by the dead. So they placed a bowl of water outside the visitation room, for visitors to purify themselves before and after paying their respects. Small flasks of oil were placed all around the bed for this purpose, too.

During the laying-out period, the family nailed cypress branches (supposedly my favorite tree) over the door as a sign of mourning. Why did they associate cypress trees with me? Because they're ugly, they're strong-smelling, and they bear no fruit. Yeah, thanks so much.

A family member placed a gold coin inside the dead person's mouth, or sometimes over the dead person's eyes. Remember, Charon didn't work for free, and nobody wanted their loved ones stuck in no-man's land because they forgot to pay the ferryman.

Sometimes they shoved a honey cake into the hands of the dead before the funeral procession—a little doggie treat for my guard dog, Cerberus. He always appreciates treats, but they're completely unnecessary. You don't need to bribe my monster-dog to get *into* Hades. Getting *out* is another matter.

STEP 2—THE *EKPHORA* (FUNERAL PROCESSION).

After about a day of hanging around the house, it was time to move the dead to their final resting place. Remember, the Greeks believed that the dead couldn't "rest" until funeral rites were finished—so, the sooner, the better. The Romans, on the other hand, laid the body out for *nine* days. Not surprisingly, they added incense and flowers—lots of it—to hide the stench.

The procession usually set out before dawn. The men of the family carried the litter with the now-shrouded body, followed by wailing women—including strangers paid to scream and cry—and maybe even some musicians. In ancient Greece, a silent funeral was an oxymoron.

Both the Greeks and the Romans either buried their dead or burned them on funeral pyres. Most preferred burning, since it represented the soul or psyche of the dead disappearing like smoke into nothingness.

At the funeral pyre, there was more wailing and frantic grieving. Some Greek leaders disliked all the drama, so they passed laws that limited the number of people who were allowed to show up at funerals and even tried to regulate wailing and face-gouging. The Romans, on the other hand, believed it was undignified for men to do anything but frown. Only Roman women were allowed to show strong emotion, but even that was discouraged.

STEP 3—THE FUNERAL.

Once the fire was a-roarin', relatives sometimes threw precious items belonging to the deceased into the flames—such as a favorite drinking cup or statue. But they symbolically broke or "killed" these things first, which totally annoyed me because, hello, who likes to receive broken gifts? Just one more insult to the king of the dead.

Anyway, precious objects weren't the only things "killed" at funerals. Animals were often sacrificed to honor the dead. In *The Iliad*, when the hero Achilles performed the rites for his beloved friend Patroclus (peh-*trahk*-liss), he went even further—he sacrificed twelve young Trojan men, along with two dogs and four horses. We're talking human sacrifice, people!

Which reminds me: If you see Achilles down here, do *not*—and I repeat, do *not*—irritate him. Things don't end well when Achilles gets angry.

When the funeral fire began to die down, mourners called out the dead's name three times as a final farewell. Finally, the fire was put out with either water or wine.

After the pyre cooled, mourners gathered the bones and ashes and put them into an urn. Then they left offerings of flowers, perfumes, wine, fruit, and oil at the graveside.

Oil was expensive, though, so family members

sometimes cheated. They would bring large jars, which made it look as though the family were being extremely generous—but inside the jars were tiny inner chambers that held the barest amount of oil. Oh, little mortals. Did you really think the king of the dead didn't know you were cheating?

By the way, no priests attended these rites. The family took care of everything. And why were there no priests? Because my people did not *have* any priests to honor the king of the underworld. No temples or cult centers, either. In fact, priests of other gods and goddesses were not *allowed* to be anywhere near a funeral, lest they become polluted by my presence. Now, is that any way to treat a king? Seriously, the outrage never ends.

STEP 4—THE CLEANSING.

In Athens—one of my people's most famous city-states— mourners had yet another ceremony for purifying the living from me and my supposed "miasma" (the bad-smelling air that surrounds the dead): Relatives dug a trench on the west side of the grave or monument and poured water into it, while chanting that the water would keep the deceased clean. They also poured myrrh—a powerful, cleansing herb—into the trench for further purification.

Again, with the insults! Hades is not a filthy place. Okay, yeah, it's dark, dank, and musty, and smells of rotten eggs, but that's not the same as "dirty."

STEP 5—THE BANQUET.

The mourners typically bathed when they got home, in yet another cleansing ritual. Afterward, they held a feast where they ate the barbecued flesh of the animals they had sacrificed. The shade of the newly deceased was believed to be present at the banquet.

But enough about rites and rules. Charon awaits. Hand over your coin so we can get across the Styx already. Oh, and don't worry if Charon doesn't speak much. I intimidate him—as I should, given that I'm his ruler. But mostly he's afraid of me because of a punishment I once called down upon him.

It happened when he rowed that meat-head hero Herakles across the Styx to my realm—even though, 1) Herakles was still alive and that's against the rules, and, 2) The brute didn't even bring a coin. Charon took him across for free because the world's strongest man scowled at him.

Yeah.

I made Charon pay for this grievous mistake by clapping him in chains for a year and a day. Take it from him, don't test me.

INTO THE GATES
OF DOOM

CAREFUL, NOW—YOU definitely do *not* want to dangle your fingers in the water of the Styx. This roiling river of muck, remember, is also called the River of Hate. All kinds of evil creepy-crawlers might pop up and try to drag you down into the putrid blackness.

You know, for such a skeletal guy, Charon really works his oar like a champ, don't you think? He got us across quickly. It's time to come on out of the boat now, so step lively.

It's good to be on the other side of the Styx. Hear that growling and snarling? That's my pet, Cerberus. One popular fantasy book featuring a boy wizard who shall not be named calls my fearsome dog "Fluffy."

Really? Cerberus is my *guard dog*. Plus, he is huge and fierce. Even his spit could kill you.

Don't believe me? Ask Medea, a ruthless sorceress who used some of Cerberus's spit when she tried to murder Theseus of Athens (the hero who killed the bull-headed monster, the Minotaur). I didn't mind Theseus, because he was a son of Poseidon, *not Zeus*. Anyway, one Roman poet claims Medea put Cerberus's saliva in the boy's wine in her assassination attempt. (It didn't work, because Theseus didn't drink it.)

How did she get my dog's poison to begin with? That son of Zeus's, the one I love to hate—Herakles—snuck down here and *stole* my guard dog on a dare. Okay, it was more like a "labor"—a job he had to do for a king—but, still. Who does he think he is?

He dragged my poor doggie into the upper world. The sunlight blinded Cerby and made him sick. As he barked and whined piteously, drool and spittle flew everywhere. Medea grabbed some of that spit for her collection of poisons. Smart girl. I like Medea because she sent so many dead my way—including her own children.

(Which reminds me: If you see Medea down here, *run!*)

The rest of my poor poochie's spit burned into the ground and turned into poisonous plants known as aconite and wolfsbane. It was believed that wolfsbane cured werewolves—or at least, kept people from turning into werewolves during the full moon. Yeah, it did that, all right—by *killing* any fool who ingested it!

So that's my long way of saying, do not stand under any of my dog's slobbering mouths when we walk by. One drop o' drool and you're a goner.

Most people picture my dog with three heads, but that is wrong, wrong, wrong. He is way cooler than that. Some poets claimed he had fifty heads and some poets called him the "hundred-headed" beast. Others described him with not only multiple heads, but with a serpent's tail, a mane of snakes, and lion's paws.

Whatever. I call him awesome.

Here, boy! Good boy! No, no, don't eat my little friend. See? He's a good dog. Very sweet when you're entering my realm. It's only when you try to *leave* that he gets a mite grouchy. That's because once you enter, you can never leave.

Ever.

But don't worry. I'll make sure he makes an exception for you.

Wait, you don't trust me? Well, then, I hope you have some doggie treats in your pockets. You might need them.

GUARDIAN OF FEARS

My people believed that Cerberus did more than just guard my gates; he protected the living from the scary dead. By making sure that none of the dead left the underworld to roam upstairs, he kept the worlds separate. "Shades" (what my people called the dead) were a scary lot and my people rather liked that my lion-pawed, multi-headed, snaky-haired beast was keeping them in their place. In other words, Cerberus was more of a comfort to the *living.*

Even so, my people believed that the shades of the dead sometimes drifted into the upper world to haunt others—especially if the dead hadn't received the proper rites. (Remember Melinoe?) But that wasn't Cerberus's fault. These shades were the ones stuck in the no-man's land of the unburied dead. When these ghosts appeared to the living, they usually demanded that something be done about their poor, unburied selves.

The first known ancient ghost story (and probably the most famous) came to us from a Roman writer named Pliny the Younger:

THE HAUNTED HOUSE OF ATHENS

The big house had a terrible reputation: At night, you could hear the sound of metal chains clanging within. Then, a phantom would appear—an old man, emaciated and filthy, with a long beard and unkempt hair. He wore shackles on his legs and chains on his wrists, and he shook them as he walked.

The family who lived in the house spent many dreadful nights lying awake in fear. Illness and eventually death overtook them, thanks to lack of sleep and a sense of constant dread. And so, the house was deserted. The person who inherited the house tried to sell or rent it, hoping to find someone who had not heard about the resident ghost.

A philosopher named Athenodorus came to Athens and needed a place to stay. When he heard the low rent price of the abandoned house, he grew suspicious and began asking questions. When he learned about the ghost, he became even more interested. He immediately rented the house. On his first night, he moved his bed to the front of the house and set himself up with writing tablets, a stylus, and a map.

He busied himself with writing in order to keep his imagination in check. At first, there was only silence. After a time, there came the sound of iron clashing, of chains clanking; yet Athenodorus did not raise his eyes or put down his stylus. Instead, he concentrated even more attentively on his work.

The din grew louder and moved ever closer. Suddenly, he realized the noise was inside the room with him! Athenodorus looked up and saw the ghost, but ignored it and went back to his writings. The ghost continued rattling its chains right over the philosopher's head.

Again, Athenodorus looked up, and this time he noticed that the ghost was moving its hand as if to beckon him. The philosopher picked up his lamp and followed the phantom. The specter walked very slowly, as if weighed down by the chains. Then it walked into the courtyard of the house and vanished. Athenodorus, now alone, plucked some grass and leaves to mark the spot where the ghost had disappeared. In the morning, he dug up the ground in that area.

There, he found bones of a dead man entwined in chains. He gathered the bones and gave them a public burial. After the rites were performed, the ghost never returned.

The story, of course, was a warning: Bury your dead correctly, and you won't have to face ghosts coming a-knocking . . . or a-clanging.

Ah, look. *Good boy, Cerby!* Cerberus has finally let us through the enormous gleaming black gates of my kingdom.

As the gates were closing behind us, you may have noticed a bunch of creatures zipping by to get outside. Those were the Cadodaemones (keh-kah-*dee*-mown-eez), evil little spirit-demons that regularly shoot out of my gates to fly into the upper world. Their job? To torture the living, usually with insanity. Good thing one didn't accidentally-on-purpose fly into *you*, eh?

FIELDS OF UGLY FLOWERS

Now that we are inside my realm, we are standing in the Fields of Asphodel, a flower meadow. My people thought asphodels were my favorite flowers. Why? Because they are pale and straggly, and because fields of them look like ghosts waving despondently in the wind.

Yeah, my people figured that I would only like "meadows of ugly." The disrespect never ends.

Anyway, that's where the common folk, the ordinary—those who were neither good nor bad—dwelled for eternity. And really, it could be worse. I mean, hanging around in a meadow of ghost-like flowers is better than being tossed into Tartaros, the pit of punishment. Soon you'll see why.

Oh look, here comes the wild red-headed fiend Empusa. She walks funny because she's got one donkey's leg and her other leg is made of bronze—which explains why she's always in a bad mood.

Because we're walking past Asphodel, she must think we're travelers, her favorite road snack. She loves to attack people on deserted byways, either eating their flesh or drinking their blood. But don't worry; she won't attack you, because I'm here.

Be sure to smile and wave politely as we pass her, though. As fearsome as Empusa is, she's got a very fragile ego. If you insult her, she will screech and wail and run away. So please, under no circumstances should you call her a "donkey-hoofed peg-leg." Seriously, don't. Her wailing always gives me a headache.

MY CATTLE RANCH

On the right, you'll see Meneotes, my cattle-keeper. What? You didn't know I owned a cattle ranch? My cows and bulls are all black (naturally), with gorgeous, gleaming coats. On one of Herakles's many unlawful trips down here, the brute stole one of my bulls and sacrificed it, leaving the blood for the ghosts to snack on.

My people believed that ghosts could only remember their lives or talk to the living if they drank blood first. So, if the living wanted to talk to the dead, they needed to bring blood for them. Why would anyone *want* to be able to talk to ghosts? Well, many heroes came down here to get "inside information" from the dead, like how to get home (Odysseus) or what the future held (Aeneas). *And* they brought their own supply of blood—in the form of sacrifices—to get the dead to start yakking.

Herakles, being the brute-brat-boy he is, didn't bother asking permission before coming down here; nor did he bring his own sacrifice for blood. He just stole one of my cows instead, the lazy bum. Meneotes rightly got angry and told him off. Herakles tackled him and broke one of his ribs. That over-muscled bully would have killed Meneotes if my wife, Persephone, hadn't stopped him.

But look, my gleaming palace emerges from the black mists! Let's head on over.

THE BLACK PALACE

I BET YOU'VE NEVER seen a cooler royal enclosure. In fact, I'm sure of it, which is why you should've brought a sweater. What did you expect—that my black palace would be warm and toasty? Kid, this is the underworld. It's always cold. Unless you're thrown into the lake of fire, of course.

As we approach the entrance, check out my orchard of pomegranate trees. Pomegranates are the sweetest, most delicious fruits in my realm. Okay, they are the *only* fruits in my realm. Still, I love them. It's thanks to the pomegranates that Persephone struck a deal to stay with me part of the year.

The rule is, if you eat something down here, you

can't go back up to the upper world, even if you're a god. Persephone ate a handful of pomegranate seeds when she was first down here, which bound her to return to my realm.

The giant owl over my orchard was once Askolophos, the man who tended my pomegranate trees. He's the one who told Demeter that her daughter had eaten from his trees and had to stay in my realm. Demeter threw a hissy fit. She hurled Askolophos to the underworld so hard he was buried under a rock. Herakles eventually moved the rock, releasing him. But Persephone stayed so mad at Askolophos for tattle-telling that when he emerged from under the rock, she sprinkled him with water from the fiery Phlegethon River, which instantly turned him into an annoying screech owl.

So now I have a screech owl for a gardener. Yeah, thanks, Persephone.

Anyway, my kingdom is a big place. I have a lot of assistants and workers. Come and meet some of them.

MY EXCELLENT FIENDISH STAFF

See that winged man over there? That is Thanatos, God of Death. Wait, you thought *I* was the god of death? No, no. I am the god of *the dead* and of my realm. Thanatos is the one who kills ya. Relax; he's only responsible for nonviolent death. Ker is the goddess of violent death. Thankfully, she's not here right now.

Standing next to Thanatos is his twin brother,

Hypnos, God of Sleep. Hypnos has wings coming out of the sides of his head. How cool is that? Sometimes he was painted with wings on his head *and* on his ankles—I guess for those times when he needs an extra lift.

Flitting above us are the Oneiroi (on-*air*-roy), the black-winged spirits of dreams. Every night they careen out of here like bats out of Hades. Sometimes they go to deliver prophetic dreams—dreams that tell the future—or dreams sent by the gods. Most of them, though, carry meaningless dreams. By the way, we get the word "nightmare" from these guys—*melas oneiros* (*mel*-ess on-*air*-ohss), "carriers of the black dream."

So the next time you have a bad dream, you can thank my dark little fluttery minions. You might even hear them flapping outside your window as you wake up. If you miss them, don't worry. They'll be back.

THE ONES WHO CALL THE SHOTS

As we pass by one of my palace's many rooms, you may catch a glimpse of the Moirae (*moy*-ray), or Fates, three ancient-looking goddesses who spin the threads of life—and death.

Even we gods are a little frightened of them. These women are tough and severe and no one—not even we Olympians—can break away from our fates once these goddesses set them.

At your birth, they spin out the threads of your future. As you live, they watch to make sure the cloth of your life is woven according to your fate. And at the end of your life, the fate of death—the Moirai Thanatoio—snips the thread, and down you come to me. I like the fate of death. She's my favorite.

Now, follow me into the throne room. I want you to meet my wife, Persephone.

THE QUEEN OF THE UNDERWORLD

Ah, there she is, accompanied by Hekate, the goddess of night, witchcraft, and magic. Hekate is yet another goddess you do not want to anger. Her specialty is coming up with terrible punishments. Once, she turned the boy Akteon into an animal, so that his hunting dogs could tear him to pieces, because Artemis, the goddess of the hunt, had found his behavior insulting.

So I suggest you be on your best behavior.

Lounging next to Hekate are the goddess's minions, female vampires known as the Lamiae (*lae*-mee-eyes). They tricked young men into following them by looking all shiny-haired and sweet-smilingly beautiful. But when the Lamiae had them in their grasp, these beautiful women turned into blood-sucking vampires who drained their prey dry. One ancient playwright claimed they got their name—which meant "gullet" in ancient Greek—because they had a habit of devouring children. Pay them no attention when they start whispering about how yummy you look, okay?

My wife is the beautiful one on the throne. Persephone is the daughter of Demeter and Zeus. You already know how she ended up down here with me for three months of the year. When she goes upstairs to her mother's world, she personifies the blossoming of spring.

Her mother, as you know, hates me; she claims that Persephone has no love for me, either. Not true. Once, a nymph named Minthe fell in love with me, and you should have seen Persephone's reaction. She tracked the little nymph down and stomped her so thoroughly into the ground that the poor thing turned into a plant. We call it *mint*.

Clearly, my wife is devoted to me. (Just don't tell her that mint is my favorite tea.)

THE QUEEN SPEAKS

Welcome, little mortal. It has been some time since a living human has dared come to visit us. Good luck making it out alive.

But before I begin, I need a little snack. Hades, dear, would you peel me a pomegranate? And pour me a cup of ambrosia? That's a sweet god—thank you.

Anyway, when I'm down here, I try to make the best of it, but I have to admit, it gets a little boring. Okay, a lot boring. Seriously, all there is to do down here is to listen to the constant moaning and wailing of the dead. While that may have been fun at first, it gets old fast.

Having visitors shakes things up a little, at least. My husband, though, immediately turns into "Grumpy McGrouchstein" whenever anyone drops in. I wish he would lighten up.

Let me tell you about some of my favorite visitors.

ORPHEUS AND HIS KILLER MUSIC

Orpheus, son of a muse and Apollo, fell madly in love with a nymph named Eurydice. Soon after their marriage, Eurydice was bitten by a snake and died.

Orpheus wound his way down here—using his music to charm Cerberus and Charon—and begged us to release Eurydice so that she could go back to the world of the living with him.

My husband, Grumpy McGrouchstein, immediately said no. But I was touched by Orpheus's devotion and charmed by his music. I pleaded his case and Grumpy relented. But only under one condition—Orpheus could not look upon his wife until they left the underworld.

And so they set out. It's a long walk to the upper world and Orpheus forced himself not to look back— even though he didn't know if his wife really was behind him, even though he couldn't wait to see her again. When he saw light, he knew they were nearly at the mouth of the cave. He was so excited! He stepped out into the light and, with his heart in his throat, turned to see his beloved finally returned to him.

But Orpheus had turned too early. Eurydice was still in the shadows of the cave—only two steps away! As he reached out to her, she melted back into the underworld.

Poor, poor boy. But that's what you get for not following the rules.

ODYSSEUS'S BRING-YOUR-OWN-BLOOD GHOST PARTY

Odysseus, king of Ithaca and star of Homer's *Odyssey*, came down here after the Trojan War because he was lost and wanted to get home to his wife, Penelope. The only person who could help him with directions was a dead seer. So he had nowhere to go but down.

Odysseus remembered that he needed blood to get the dead to talk, so he brought two lambs with him, sacrificed them, and poured their blood into a trench. Lots of ghosts crowded around the still-steaming ruby-colored blood, wanting a sip, but O-man wouldn't let anyone drink until the dead seer came. After slurping the gooey stuff, the seer finally told Odysseus how to get home.

While he was down here, Odysseus also saw his mom, but she didn't recognize him. Once she had some blood, though, she got all weepy and told him that she died from missing him. Talk about a guilt trip.

Anyway, he also spoke with Achilles, the hero of the Trojan War, who told him that being dead was so miserable, he'd rather be a poor peasant in the upper world than the king of the underworld. To this day, my husband swears he'd like to crush Achilles under his heel for that insult.

THESEUS, PIRITHOUS, AND THE LEFTOVER BUTT

One day, two heroes—Theseus and Pirithous—decided that they were so awesome, only the daughters of Zeus were worthy of them. Pirithous helped Theseus steal a very young Helen (the one who would become Helen of Troy), though her brothers later rescued her. Then Theseus helped Pirithous come down here to steal ... me! That's right; Pirithous decided that even though I was married to the king of the dead, taking me for himself was a good idea. The fool.

Anyway, the pair came down to the underworld and visited my husband, waiting for the opportunity to steal me away. Hades pretended not to know why they had come. (Really, guys? Did ya think he couldn't tell?) He bade them sit down on two beautiful thrones. Honored, they sat . . . and immediately lost all their memories. My husband had tricked them into sitting in the Chairs of Forgetfulness.

My husband's most-hated nephew, Herakles, heard about their predicament when he was here to steal Cerberus, so he came by the palace to rescue them. Herakles pulled and pulled, using all his strength, but he

could not get Theseus out of the chair. Finally, with one mighty yank, he succeeded—leaving most of Theseus's backside stuck to the throne! That's right. He left his tushy down here! See that chair across the room with the fluffy two-sided pillow on it? It's not a pillow. Anyway, that story later became the myth about why Theseus's people had such flat butts.

Herakles then turned to help Pirithous, but he could not pull him off the throne. When an earthquake hit, Herakles and Theseus ran away, leaving Pirithous down here. He's still stuck in the Chair of Forgetfulness—as he should be, for daring to think himself worthy of me.

PSYCHE AND THE SEARCH FOR MY MAGIC CREAM

In the Roman era, there was a beautiful young princess named Psyche (whose name means "the soul"). Venus, the Roman Goddess of Love, grew jealous of the girl and sent her son Cupid to make Psyche fall in love with a loathsome man.

But Cupid fell in love with Psyche instead. He didn't want her to know that he was a god, though, so he only came to her at night and only in the dark. After Cupid made Psyche promise never to look upon him, he took her away and they married secretly. But Psyche's jealous sisters told her that she was married to a monster. If he wasn't a monster, they said, then why wasn't she allowed to look at him?

Eventually, Psyche snuck a peek at her husband. She was so shocked at his beauty that she accidentally spilled hot oil from her lamp and burned him. Cupid—furious, and in a lot of pain—flew away.

Psyche was determined to win him back. So she set off after Cupid, finally going to his mother. But the goddess of love can be hateful sometimes, and Venus punished the girl by forcing her to do many seemingly impossible things. One of them was to come down here and steal some of my beauty (as if!).

Psyche eventually made it down here to the underworld and explained to me that the goddess of love wanted to steal my beauty. I told her I couldn't give her my beauty, but I would sprinkle some of it into a cream that she could take back to Venus. That sweet soul-girl was very grateful.

Once in the upper world, Psyche thought she'd try some of the cream herself, opened the box, and promptly passed out. (Yes, I have killer looks, if I do say so myself.) Cupid found her, revived her, and zipped up with her to Mount Olympus. He asked my father, Zeus, to help get his mother off their backs and Zeus agreed. Zeus called all the Olympians and declared that Cupid and Psyche were officially married. He even gave Psyche ambrosia to make her immortal.

Thanks to Zeus's proclamation, Cupid (love) and Psyche (soul) are always together. No thanks to the goddess of love, mind you.

AENEAS'S HUNT FOR HIS DAD IN ELYSIUM

All the other sons of gods that visited us here in the underworld were Greek; Aeneas was Roman. By this time, most of our ancient people believed that a hero wasn't a "true" hero unless he made a little trip down here to the underworld. My grumpy husband is convinced they do it just to torture him.

By the way, the Romans called our realm "Dis," which Hades thinks is disrespectful. So don't "diss" him about it, okay?

Anyway, off Aeneas went. He made his way past Charon by showing off a solid gold tree branch that he planned to give me as an offering. Wasn't that a nice present?

Then Aeneas gave poor Cerberus something to make him fall asleep so he could sneak in. He eventually made it all the way to Elysium, where heroes and the good lived in the afterlife. Aeneas wanted to know what the future held in store for him. He found his dad and asked him. Well, the old man—living large in our "happy place"—not only told Aeneas about his life, but also predicted the future glory of his descendants and all of Rome. Yay, Aeneas.

But I must stop here, as I have pressing matters to attend to—namely, counting how many more days I have to spend in this hell-hole before spring. You understand, don't you, dear?

Oh. Ahem. Yes. Thank you, my queen. And now, it is time to make people suffer . . . er, I mean, witness the judging of the newly dead.

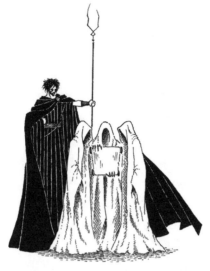

THE HALL OF JUDGMENT

FOLLOW ME INTO MY GREAT HALL where we decide the fates of the dead. What fun!

I have some help on this job, though I should mention that I am not particularly fond of my assistants, the judges of the dead. And why is that? Because they, too, are sons of Zeus.

I know. Will I never escape my little brother's meddling?

Zeus claims that he *had* to get his sons involved in the judging of the dead because he'd heard that some undeserving souls were sneaking into the Isle of the Blessed, the other name for Elysium. Vile rumors, all of them. Nevertheless, he used that accusation to stick his nose into my business and appoint his sons, the Greek kings Rhadamanthys, Minos, and Aiakos, to "help me" with the judging.

I'm sorry, but you don't see me sending my minions up there to "help" polish Zeus's lightning bolts or fluff up his storm clouds, now, do you?

My little brother claimed that his sons deserved to be judges because they were good kings when they were alive. They introduced laws and made sure their people followed them. Still, what nerve.

But I was stuck with them, so I had Rhadamanthys (rad-uh-*man*-thuhs) judge the dead who come from the east; Aiakos (ah-*ee*-ah-kos) handles the dead who come from Europe; and Minos makes the final call if either of his brothers can't decide.

Ultimately, though, I can override all three of them. And often I do. Just because I can.

FIRST UP: THE NEITHER-GOOD-NOR-BAD GUYS

If you recall, those who didn't do anything good or bad end up drifting around in the Fields of Asphodel. Those souls are pretty easy to judge. They're the ones whose lives were so boring that the judges fell asleep when they looked them over.

Some of my people claimed, though, that after a while these souls become purified in the Lethe, the River of Forgetfulness, and that they get another shot at living a better life by being reborn. Hopefully, they learn to start doing some good in the world.

The good people—the heroes, philosophers, and virtuous ones—are sent to Elysium. You'd think there would be lots of clapping and shouting with joy when a shade gets sent to the Isle of the Blessed, but there isn't. Why? Because these people are typically quite humble. Bragging is a sign of hubris or excessive pride. We gods *hate* humans who show hubris, so it's no surprise that the blessed are quietly grateful.

The best part is when one of the judges sends someone to Tartaros. The wailing and the gnashing that follows the pronouncement, the begging and screaming that it involves. . . . Ahhhhh, it often soothes me to sleep, you know.

Oh, look, here comes a politician now. We'll just go ahead and plan on tossing him into the pit.

OFF TO THE PIT OF MISERY

As we approach Tartaros, you will notice that the piteous wails and moans of the suffering get even louder. I think of it as our Misery Orchestra.

Tartaros, if you recall, was the pit where we Olympians bound the Titans when we overthrew them. Nobody wanted those baby-eating Titans to sneak out of their stone jail, so we installed fulltime guards around it. Called Hekatonkheires (hek-uh-*tong*-kuh-reez), they are fierce giants with one hundred arms and fifty heads each. The monsters' oddness scared the Titans back when they were the original gods, so the Titans imprisoned them in Tartaros. Just because they didn't like the way they looked! I'm telling you, our parent gods were harsh.

Anyway, Zeus let the Hekatonkheires out during the war with the Titans. They helped us win by throwing one hundred enormous rocks at a time at our enemies, after which we hired them as guards to keep their previous jailers jailed. Sweet justice, eh?

Also, we love the Hekatonkheires because they are great in the outfield during our annual monsters-vs.-demons softball game.

Over time, my people grew to believe that there were many levels for the wicked over that original pit. But getting sent to Tartaros isn't always an eternal sentence. Some of the wicked make up for their evil deeds and actually make it out. But it isn't easy. Especially for murderers. After a period of time (maybe even decades and decades), murderers can find the ghost of the one they killed and beg for forgiveness. If the ghost forgives them, then they can leave Tartaros. If the ghost is still angry, back they go. Some ghosts stay angry for a very, very long time.

Those who killed their mothers or fathers get special treatment from the Erinyes (air-ee-*nee*-yez)—sometimes called the Furies—female monsters of revenge. Erinyes were often depicted as ugly, crazed women with wings, draped in black robes of mourning. They usually have hissing snakes wrapped all over them, too. These gals don't just wait until their victims die to begin torturing them. In the upper world, the Erinyes used to screech and chase after their victims until they went insane.

A famous case was Orestes, who killed his mother, Clytemnestra, in a revenge murder. She had killed his father—her husband, Agamemnon—who had killed their daughter Iphigenia. Yeah, the family that killed together, stayed together—in Tartaros, anyway—forever.

But it's not just murder that we gods despise. There are certain crimes that bring out the worst in us. Come find out what some of them are.

SISYPHUS: TORTURE BY ROCK

See that man over there pushing a giant rock up a hill? That's Sisyphus. He's got to push that boulder up that mountain using every ounce of his strength. When he finally gets it to the top, guess what happens—nothing! The boulder rolls all the way back down again and Sisyphus has to start all over. Every day. For eternity.

Yeah, remember that punishment when you think you have too much homework. It could always be worse, kid.

So what did Sisyphus do to earn such a miserable punishment? He messed with us gods, that's what.

First, he was a tattletale. Sisyphus saw Zeus run

away with a pretty river nymph. When the girl's enraged river-god father demanded to know where they'd gone, Sisyphus had the nerve to bargain with the river-god: "I'll only tell you," he said, "if you give me a spring of fresh bubbly water in the middle of my city."

"Fine," the river-god said, and when he was done, Sisyphus told him where the couple had gone.

The nymph's daddy chased Zeus down and my little brother got so scared that he turned himself into a rock and changed the nymph into an island. What a baby, am I right?

Anyway, soon after, Zeus sent me a message telling me to haul Sisyphus down here. First of all, what am I—his errand-boy? I sent Thanatos, the god of death, instead. Thanatos, not wanting to take any chances, brought chains for Sisyphus's wrists.

Sisyphus pretended not to know how they worked, so he asked the god of death to demonstrate. Thanatos clasped them on his own wrists. Sisyphus promptly threw him in a closet and sauntered away.

Okay, I love my god of death, but *really*, Thanatos? Anybody could've seen that trick coming from a mile away. Except for Atlas—he might've fallen for it. (Look up the stories of Atlas the Titan and you'll see what I mean, kid.) There's another version of the story where I'm the one Sisyphus tricked. Um, no. It was Thanatos. I swear.

Anyway, with Thanatos chained up, there was no death. Warriors were getting chopped up on the battlefield, but they didn't die. It wasn't pretty. Also, it made me furious. Nobody escapes death and my underworld! Yet suddenly *everyone* was escaping it.

Ares, the god of war, was particularly incensed. How could there be a victor in warfare if nobody *died*? So Ares hunted down Sisyphus and made him release Thanatos. At that point, Sisyphus surrendered and Thanatos brought him to me.

But Sisyphus was determined to get out of my kingdom. So right before he died, he secretly instructed his wife to give him no burial rites. "Just throw my naked body into the city square," he told her. She did.

Once down here, he snuck into our throne room and put on a big act about being dishonored. He begged to be allowed to return to the upper world to make sure his body got the proper rites. My soft-hearted wife, Persephone, fell for the story and let him go.

Once "upstairs," he decreed that he was never going back to the underworld. After a while, I caught on (what can I say—it's busy down here) and I demanded that he be brought back. Hermes dragged Sisyphus back down to be punished by having to push that boulder up a hill . . . forever.

Lesson: You can't escape death. Also, don't make us gods look bad.

TORTURING TANTALUS

The son of Zeus (yes, *another* one), King Tantalus of Sipylos, was one of his father's favorites. Zeus often shared his secrets with the fool—I mean, the mortal—and even allowed him to drink nectar and eat ambrosia. But Tantalus did not honor these gifts; he spilled Zeus's secrets and shared the god's sacred food with other mortals.

Worse, he tried to trick the gods at our own table on Mount Olympus. Tantalus killed his son Pelops, chopped him up, and served him as stew to us. Why? Who knows? Probably just so he could say, *Nah-nah-nah-boo-boo, you ate my son and didn't even know it!*

We all knew what he was up to, of course, so none of us touched the food. Except for my mother-in-law.

Demeter claimed to be so despondent over Persephone being with me that she absentmindedly ate a portion of Pelops's shoulder. (Like a true drama queen, everything had to be about her. Also, shouldn't the goddess of plants be a vegetarian? Just wonderin'.)

Zeus in particular was outraged by Tantalus and his attempted trick—probably because one of his sons proved himself a fool yet again. Anyway, he had one of the Moirae (Fates) collect the body parts and bring Pelops back to life. Hephaestus created a new shoulder bone made of ivory to make up for Demeter's mistake.

As punishment, Tantalus was sent to Tartaros for a particularly clever and cruel punishment (if I do say so, myself). He stood in a lake of crystal-clear water, but whenever he grew thirsty and reached down for a sip, the water receded. Also, a luscious fruit tree hung over his head, but whenever he tried to eat, the fruit moved just out of reach. For all eternity, he would be inches from cool, clean water to slake his thirst and sweet, juicy fruit to sate his hunger. Tantalus's eternal punishment is to be tempted but never satisfied—to be endlessly *tantalized*.

Lesson: Do not mess with us gods. Also, just to be clear, do not sacrifice humans and eat them.

PROUD PROMETHEUS

Prometheus was one of the good-guy Titans. He helped us Olympians fight against the bad-guy Titans, so he got to hang out in the upper world. One day, Prometheus was playing with some clay and decided to fashion humans out of it. He breathed into his creation, giving humans life.

Zeus didn't much care, except Prometheus took it too far. The Titan had a soft spot for his creations and he saw that they were offering up the best portions of sacrificed bulls to the gods—even if they were starving.

"No, no, that won't do," he told the humans. "Here's what you should do. Divide this bull into two portions. In one bag, place the bones and cover them up with the fat. In another, put everything else that you can eat or use, such as skin for leather."

Prometheus then told Zeus to choose one of the bags. Even though Zeus says he knew what the Titan was doing, he chose the one with the bones and fat.

Personally, I think he wasn't paying attention and just grabbed the one that looked the biggest, as my greedy little brother is wont to do. Anyway, Zeus had been tricked. Now humans got to keep the best parts of their sacrifices while giving the gods only the useless bones and fat.

Strike one for Prometheus.

Zeus never liked to be tricked. To punish the humans, he took away their fire. Humans could not live without fire, and they became like animals again. Prometheus felt sorry for them, so he stole some of Zeus's fire and brought it down to mankind in a hollow plant.

Strike two.

As punishment, Zeus created a human woman named Pandora and gave her to Prometheus. (Presumably, there were no human women yet, which makes no sense. But just go with it, okay?) Not trusting Zeus, Prometheus did not accept this gift of the first woman. He gave her to his brother Epimetheous, instead.

Strike three.

Earlier, being a champion of humans, Prometheus had taken all the evils in the world and sealed them in a giant jar so that humans could live happily and peacefully. Zeus found the jar and told Hermes to bring it to Pandora as a "gift." Then he was instructed to tell her, "Do *not* open this jar."

To be fair, how would you feel if one of your parents brought you a gleaming package and said, "This is for you! But you can never open it." What's the first thing you'd want to do?

Open it, of course!

Which is what Pandora did, releasing all the evil of the world to haunt humanity forever and ever. But even that wasn't enough for Zeus. He was still so mad, he decided he needed to punish Prometheus even more. So he had the Titan shackled to a rock. Every day a giant eagle attacks him by eating his liver straight out of his writhing body. Every night his liver regenerates, just in time for the eagle to devour it again the next day.

Some say Prometheus was bound on top of an earthly mountain, but that's not the case. It all happened—and still takes place—right here in Tartaros. Other storytellers claimed that Herakles released Prometheus, freeing him from his eternal punishment. But those are just rumors. He's still down here. Don't you hear that terrible wailing of pain and misery? Yeah, that's him.

Lesson: Don't make Zeus look bad.

Other famous losers down here include one guy named Ixeon who is tied to a fiery wheel that spins endlessly (he tried to steal Zeus's wife) and the daughters of Danaus, who are doomed to fill up a water jar with cups punctured with holes. They got that particular water torture for killing their husbands on their daddy's orders.

I must admit, Tartaros is my favorite place in all of the upper or under worlds. There's always a show going on, filled with pain, misery, and wailing. I mean, what more could a god of the dead wish for?

OF MONSTERS
AND CURSES

SEE THOSE GIANT one-eyed monsters just hanging around the fire pits of Tartaros? They are Cyclopes, immortal giants who have one huge orb-like eye. Do not confuse these gods/monsters with the Cyclops that Odysseus fought in *The Odyssey*. That monster—Polyphemus—was the son of Poseidon and wasn't too bright. Plus, he wasn't immortal.

The Cyclopes (they have the added "e" at the end) are gods, and brothers to the hundred-armed Hekatonkheires. We Olympians also released them from Tartaros during the Titanic war. In gratitude, they gave gifts to my brothers and me. To Zeus, they gave lightning bolts. To Poseidon, they gave a trident.

And to me, they gave a helmet of invisibility.

Sometimes my gift was called the "cap" of invisibility. Seriously? Caps are what baseball players wear. Caps are cute. Caps are silly. The king of the underworld does not wear a "cap." It's a *helmet*, people. You wouldn't call Poseidon's trident a "shrimp fork," would you? Or Zeus's lightning bolts, "sparklers"? So don't let me hear you say "cap." Furthermore, I don't want to hear anything about some wizard-boy's "Cloak of Invisibility," either. Mine came first.

This is the same *helmet* of invisibility, by the way, that I lent to the hero Perseus (another son of Zeus; sigh) so that he could sneak up on the monster Medusa to slay her. If you recall, Medusa was so ugly that if you took one look into her snaky-haired face, you turned to stone. Her two sisters were sometimes considered inhabitants of my underworld because they're evil storm-spirits who cause shipwrecks at sea.

Because they cause so much death and destruction, I welcome them here anytime.

CURSES AND MORE CURSES

The ancient Greeks and Romans may have been afraid of death and my realm, but that didn't stop them from invoking me—and the rest of us dark gods—for help in cursing their enemies. Curses, spells, and magic were big business in my day.

And, yeah, some magic was "nice," like spells for

love. But most magic spells had not-so-nice purposes. Many curses, in fact, often called for the complete and utter destruction of the enemies' physical, emotional, and spiritual selves.

The most popular way to curse someone was by scratching words on a thin sheet of lead where you spelled out—in delicious detail—all the horrible things you wanted to happen to your enemy. You moderns call them "curse tablets." Sometimes the lead sheets were rolled and bound up with hair from the intended victim (always a nice touch). They were often pierced with iron nails, too.

Occasionally people nailed their curses to temple walls—especially if they were beseeching a particular god for help in smiting someone. Mostly, though, people either buried the curse tablets or threw them into lakes, springs, or wells. The deeper they went, people figured, the faster we underworld gods would see them and set the curses into motion.

EXAMPLES FROM REAL CURSE TABLETS

Here's one fairly mild curse from the Roman era by someone who wanted the "Blue team" of charioteers to lose a race:

[B]lind every limb and every sinew of Victoricus, the charioteer of the Blue team . . . and of the

horses he is about to race. . . . Bind their legs, their onrush, their bounding, their running, blind their eyes so they cannot see and twist their soul and heart so that they cannot breathe. Just as this rooster has been bound by its feet, hands and head, so bind the legs and hands and head and heart of Victoricus, the charioteer of the Blue team, for tomorrow.

That guy must have put some serious money on the Blue team losing. But cursing the horses, too? Way harsh.

Curses against opponents in a court of law were also popular. Here's one from Athens, aimed at a whole slew of people caught up in a lawsuit:

Theagenes the butcher. I bind his tongue, his soul and the speech he is practicing. Pyrrhias. I bind his tongue, his soul and the speech he is practicing. I bind the wife of Pyrrhias, her tongue and soul. I also bind Kerkion, the butcher, and Dokimos, the butcher, their tongues, their souls and the speech they are practicing. I bind Kineas, his tongue, his soul and the speech he is practicing with Theagenes. And Pherekles. I bind his tongue, his soul and the evidence that he gives for Theagenes . . .

Did the curse work? Did the guy win his lawsuit? Maybe if you see him down here, you can ask. Yeah, he'll be down here in Tartaros. Cursing that many people guaranteed it.

Some tablets were aimed at strangers. For example, curse tablets have been found addressed to "the one who stole my cloak" or "the one who took my pig." Sometimes wax or clay dolls with pins in them accompanied the curse tablets, such as a little clay figurine with bound hands and pins inserted into its eyes, mouth, chest, stomach, and feet. This figurine was someone's love rival and the curse was aimed at completely destroying her. Clearly, when it came to love and war, my people played to *win*.

My favorites, though, were the ones that dared to threaten me and the other gods. I mean, seriously? Here's one by man who wanted us to convince the girl he loved to fall for him. Let's break down his foolishness, shall we?

I entrust this binding spell to you, gods of the underworld. . . .

So far, so good. Respectful, anyway. The spell goes on to identify the girl and how he wants her to act.

If you ignore me and fail to carry out quickly what I tell you . . . Hades and Earth [will not] continue to exist.

Whoa, that escalated quickly. Did he just threaten me with extinction?

Do not ignore me but act very quickly for I have commanded you.

Oh . . . stupid, stupid mortal.

This guy was *commanding* me? Clearly, he didn't know how we worked. Needless to say, none of us helped him. And when he arrived in the underworld, we threw him into Tartaros not only for cursing others, but for hubris—excessive pride—in daring to think that he could command us gods to do his bidding.

We gods could be appealed to, sacrificed to, and bargained with. We could be worshipped, honored, and celebrated. But commanded to obey? I don't think so.

SPEAKING OF WORSHIP, WHY DIDN'T THEY?

. . . Worship me more, that is. As unbelievable as it sounds, there were hardly any priests of Hades and few cult centers devoted to me. Even fewer statues and paintings celebrated my glory.

What was the deal?

Persephone said I should take that as a sign of people's great fear of me, which is a compliment . . . sort of. Still, it rankled that there were temples dedicated to just about every minor god known to man but so few for *me*. I mean, even Herakles had a cult center! At his temples they honored stupidity—er, I mean, brute strength. Gladiators in Rome even had special shrines devoted to that half-man, half-god meat-head.

I should've gotten at least that much, don't you think?

And, okay, occasionally my people tried. Your archaeologists (my buddy Anubis—the ancient Egyptian god of death and embalming—calls them "dirt-diggers") recently uncovered what they are calling a "gateway to hell" in the ancient city of Hierapolis in Turkey. They uncovered a Roman-era temple complex that the Romans called Plutonium, or "Pluto's Gate."

It was basically a gigantic hole in the ground that spewed toxic gas. So the Romans built a temple to me near it.

Yeah, thanks. No, really, you shouldn't have.

Where were the gifts, flowers, incense, gold, and trinkets my brothers got on a regular basis?

Instead, my so-called temple was more of a tourist site. It overlooked a giant hole in the ground that released vapors that could *kill* you. In describing this temple, one ancient writer said, "This space is full of a vapor so misty and dense that one can scarcely see the ground. Any animal that passes inside meets instant death." For fun, this guy threw a couple of sparrows into the area so that he could watch them drop dead as they flew.

Also, the priests of the temple (yay—finally, priests for me!) would send live animals to a cave near the toxic hole, just so they could drag them out dead a little while later.

Which, okay, I've got to admit, was kind of cool. But, seriously. Where was the gold? Where was the respect?

ONWARD TO THE FIELDS OF ELYSIUM, THE "HAPPY" PLACE

SADLY, WE MUST NOW LEAVE Tartaros and move to one of the least exciting areas of my realm—Elysium. Sometimes called the Elysian Fields or Isle of the Blessed, this is the place where the boring people go—er, I mean, the good people.

Originally, Homer claimed that Elysium was only for heroes—the sons and daughters of gods. Over time, the concept changed, allowing "virtuous" people to end up in Elysium, too.

But then it got even more complicated—on top of a level for heroes and a different location for average "good guys," there was also a place where those who had undergone a special ritual called "the Mysteries" went.

But that wasn't the end of it, either. The Greek philosopher Plato claimed that Elysium wasn't even in my realm but in the heavens! The Roman writer and politician Cicero claimed to have identified it in the stars, in the Milky Way galaxy.

Really, guys? The one nice thing in my realm and you try to take it away from me and throw it up into the *skies*?

I blame Zeus.

I also blame my little brother for another dastardly trick in the skies. The planet Pluto—named after yours truly (the Roman version)—was recently downgraded to planetoid or dwarf planet. Your astronomers claim it used to be a moon belonging to the planet Neptune (Roman for Poseidon), my *other* younger brother. Will the indignities never end?

Meanwhile, the largest planet in our solar system is named Jupiter, Zeus's Roman name. Gee, what a surprise.

I take comfort, however, in knowing that Jupiter—the fifth planet from the sun—is really nothing more than a giant gasbag. Just like Zeus.

THE LAND OF HEROES

As we approach Elysium, you will notice that the air smells fresher and cleaner and that sunshine seems to bathe everything in a soft, warm glow.

Nice, eh?

It kind of makes me want to puke.

What can I say? I prefer the darkness and chill of the rest of my realm—which is why I'm going to keep our little tour here short and sweet.

Let us start with the heroes and get their annoying sense of superiority out of the way. Supposedly, this is where heroes get to live "untouched by sorrow" and where they're wreathed in everlasting honor and glory.

As if these brats of my brothers' weren't already full of themselves.

Anyway, you might notice that the closer we get, the warmer it is. If Elysium seems familiar to you, that's probably because it looks like a postcard of a beautiful island. This "Isle" is full of golden sunshine, ripe fruit, and warm breezes. It never snows or rains. Everybody is always happy.

Borrrrrring.

It's also a place where these heroes get to live "immortal lives." Except they're dead. Yeah. Just go with it.

Achilles is here (remember, he's a bit of a hot-head, so don't rile him—also, don't step on his heels), as is his beloved Patroclus. Odysseus, along with his wife Penelope and son Telemachus, are here, too.

And, of course, the man I love to hate also resides in this pretty, pretty place—Herakles. Some stories claim that he went up to Olympus, but don't listen to them. Personally, I thought he belonged in Tartaros to deal with that outsized ego of his . . . but nobody asked me.

Oh, see that pretty white tree over there? It was once a nymph named Leuke, who was my girlfriend before Persephone. After Leuke died, I turned her into a white poplar so that she could hang out in this pretty place forever. My wife, Persephone, if you recall, has a grove of black poplars. When she visits Elysium, she pretends not to see Leuke's tree.

Can we move on now? Because, seriously, I cannot be in this place of so-called heroes for long before I'm seized with a mad desire to send them all to Tartaros, just on principle.

WHERE THE "VIRTUOUS" WENT

As we move into the second level of Elysium, you may be tempted to crawl into one of those hammocks hanging between palm trees. Don't. You might not want to leave, and then I'd be forced to send Thanatos after you. There are no shortcuts, kid. You still have to go through the other levels of my world and get judged to see if you are worthy of these coconut trees and hammocks.

Even though this level is boring, too, this part of Elysium is the most interesting to me. Why? Because it shows how my people's beliefs about "justice" and "goodness" evolved. Originally, as I said before, only heroes came to Elysium. But then people seemed to realize the unfairness of that—I mean, you can't help who your parents are, right? Just because one of the gods (usually Zeus) sired a kid, seemed like a weak reason for them to be eternally blessed.

What if you were helpful, kind, and fair? Shouldn't there be some reward for the average good guy? That's where Elysium for the "virtuous ones" came in.

My three judges of the dead and me, of course, judged who got to loll on this isle. Interestingly, many philosophers made it here, like that troll-like man over there. His name is Socrates. Oh, don't worry, I'm not insulting him. He likes to joke about his ugliness.

Socrates had one of the greatest minds of my people. Some credit him with being one of the founders of Western philosophy. Unfortunately, you moderns don't have any of his writings—you know of him only from the writings of other philosophers such as Plato and Xenophon.

Socrates was called a "gadfly" because he constantly asked stinging questions that made people—especially politicians—uncomfortable. He wrote about the nature of virtue, knowledge, and politics. He also invented a form of analysis called the "Socratic method," which involved asking lots of questions.

In case he comes over, you should know two things: 1) If he offers you a glass of wine, refuse it. He famously drank poisoned wine to kill himself after receiving a death sentence from the Athenian rulers. And, 2) Avoid asking him any questions. Why? Because of that whole Socratic Method thing. He can't help himself—he'll return your question with a question. I'll give you an example. Once I brought a modern young man here and forgot to warn him about Socrates. Still unused to being dead, he asked the great philosopher, "Excuse me, sir, what time do you have?"

Socrates answered, "Can you 'have' time?" and "What is time?" and "How did you know it was time to ask that question?"

Whenever the young man tried to answer, the old goat came back with, "Why do you say that?" or "How do you know that?" or "What would happen if you . . . ?" and so on and so on. Rumor is that the poor guy finally turned into a pillar of salt out of frustration.

PLATO'S PERFECT WORLD

Another famous inhabitant of Elysium is a philosopher named Plato. Founder of a famous school of philosophy in Athens called "The Academy," Plato was also a key figure in ancient philosophy. It's only through his writings that we know what Socrates believed, though it's hard to tell whether Plato was really just using Socrates's name to talk about his *own* beliefs. He also wrote about nature and virtue, as well as politics and mathematics.

Plato is most famous for his "Platonic ideal," a theory that said that everything in the world is only a flawed version of its true, "perfect" form that exists in some abstract reality. Got that?

No? It doesn't matter. You *do* need to know this: If you have a conversation with Plato, do not bring up the name Aristotle. He was once Plato's favorite student, but they began to disagree on some key points. Even so, when Plato was dying, Aristotle assumed that he would take over the school. He was crushed when Plato named someone else as his successor. So Aristotle started a competing school. The only time you'll feel a chill in Elysium is if those two accidentally bump into each other.

THE GUY SECRETLY RESPONSIBLE FOR ALL YOUR HOMEWORK

That bearded guy over there is the famous philosopher Aristotle. Like Socrates and Plato, Aristotle is also considered one of the founding philosophers of the Western tradition—only he expanded his focus from mere ideas to "sciences." He wrote about biology, geology, astronomy, botany, zoology, mathematics, politics, and just about everything else you can imagine.

He's famous for formalizing a type of thinking that we now call "logic." This was his famous example of deductive reasoning:

If all humans are mortal
and all Greeks are humans,
then all Greeks are mortal.

So he's the one to thank for all the "if/then" word problems you get in math. He was also the first to classify living things into biological groups . . . which means, he's also the one to thank for all that memorization in biology. Wait, maybe I should stop telling you about all his accomplishments—I wouldn't want you to be mean to the guy who is responsible for all your homework. I mean, we *are* in Elysium—the happy place—after all.

Let's just say he was a genius and leave it at that, okay?

Oh, and by the way, Aristotle also tutored a famous young prince who would later be known as Alexander the Great.

Other famous ancient philosophers you might see here include Epicurus, who believed that the key to happiness was living simply and avoiding extremes, and Zeno of Citium, who invented Stoicism.

Epicurus also came up with a theory that all matter was made of tiny invisible atoms—which is pretty impressive, given that he thought of this 2,500 years before the invention of microscopes!

Zeno's Stoic philosophy taught that pain came from extreme emotions, so humans needed to learn to manage their perceptions and actions to keep emotions stable. So, for example, if your friend took your favorite marker without asking, you would tell yourself that it wasn't a big deal. Under no circumstance would you act like the Lamiae and try to drink all of your friend's blood in retaliation.

Wait, that wouldn't occur to you? Wow, who knew you modern younglings were so "Stoic"?

I must be spending too much time in Tartaros.

Zeno, unfortunately, didn't think much about us gods—neither accepting nor denying our existence. But he made it into Elysium nonetheless. (I normally would've thrown him in Tartaros for daring to question us gods, but whatever. I had a soft moment.)

Lots of artists made it here, too, including the famous Greek sculptor Praxiteles and the Roman architect Vitruvius; playwrights such as Sophocles, Aeschylus, Euripides, and Aristophanes; brilliant scientists and mathematicians like Archimedes, Euclid, and Hypatia. It was a brainiac's dream!

And I know that this is hard to believe, but even some politicians made it here, such as Solon, an early Greek leader who came up with laws that formed the foundation of democracy. Also, Athenian statesman Pericles, a big advocate of democracy, and his consort Aspasia found themselves in the Isle of the Blessed.

But one of the more fascinating characters in Elysium was a guy named Pythagoras. I'd introduce you to him but he's not here right now.

He was recently reincarnated as a lentil.

BEANS, BEANS ARE GOOD FOR YOUR SOUL

When you take geometry, you'll hear about Pythagoras. That's because he pretty much invented it. As a mathematician, Pythagoras believed that all of life could be understood through the harmony of numbers and music. He and his followers also believed that souls got reborn again and again—into human, animal, and even vegetative form—until the soul was purified and became immortal.

As a result, he had strict rules about what he and his followers could or could not eat. No meat. And definitely no beans.

Why beans? No one knows exactly, though some guess Pythagoras believed that reincarnated souls lived inside them. You wouldn't want to accidentally eat the departed souls of your friends, now, would you?

So seriously did his followers take this rule about avoiding beans that, according to one story, a group of Pythagoreans once let themselves be killed by an army rather than run through a field of beans to escape.

I guess they were afraid they might trample on Grandma, or something.

According to another story, Pythagoras once saw a man beating a dog. "Stop!" he yelled. "That dog is my former friend. I recognize his voice!"

He wasn't the only Greek philosopher to believe in reincarnation, though. Plato did, too. He believed that souls in Elysium drank from the Lethe—the River of Forgetfulness—before they were reborn into a new self. The idea was that you kept trying to be better and better with every reincarnation until you reached ultimate goodness or purity.

Still, Pythagoras was my favorite. How can you not love a guy who stuck to his beliefs even when people in his own time thought they didn't amount to a hill of beans?

THE POWER OF BEANS IN ANCIENT RITUAL

Beans also played a big role in an annual Roman festival called Lemuria. Every May, Roman houses needed to be cleansed of fearful or angry ghosts. The restless dead, called *lemures*, could only be appeased by offerings of beans.

So, over the three days of the festival, the head of the household—usually the father—got up at midnight and walked barefoot throughout the house, throwing black beans over his shoulder and chanting, "With these beans, I redeem me and mine." He had to do this *nine* times. When he was done, the rest of the household clashed bronze plates and cups while repeating, "Ghosts of my fathers and ancestors, be gone!" They had to do this nine times as well. Remember, they did this for three nights. Every year.

No Roman worth his or her salt would skip this

ritual. Who knew what the ghosts would do if they didn't get their beans?

Interestingly, many Romans were named after beans—Cicero's name meant "chickpea," *Lentulus* meant "lentils," *Fabius* referred to fava beans, and *Piso* was related to the word for "peas."

Yes, the Romans loved their beans.

Which reminds me: Did you know an ancient guy invented the first whirlpool bath?

Yeah. He got into a tub after eating beans for dinner. (Clearly, he was not a Pythagorean.)

EVEN VIRGIL GOT ON THE REINCARNATION BOAT

By the time the Roman hero Aeneas traveled to my realm, it was clear that the Romans, too, had begun to accept the idea of reincarnation. That means most ancients began to view my realm as a stopover, which was fine by me. It was getting too crowded down here, anyway. I didn't have a problem with folks heading out.

Persephone, if you remember, told you about Aeneas and his journey to Hades in chapter four. Aeneas is the hero from the Roman epic *The Aeneid*, by the poet Virgil. It's a heroic story "in the tradition of Homer" (which just means Virgil copied Homer's style), all about how Aeneas goes on an epic journey to found Rome, yada, yada, yada.

What was different about Aeneas was *where* he

found the person he came to see—his dad, Anchises. All the other visiting heroes, if you recall, were either on the edges of my palace or in the Fields of Asphodil.

Aeneas's father was living large in Elysium, which makes *The Aeneid* the only ancient epic that takes us to that "blessed" place. Anchises described Elysium as lush with green "plains of pleasure" and a soft lavender sky.

He also lectured his son about what happened in my realm. Whether by water, fire, or wind, all souls were eventually cleansed, he told him, even if it took a thousand years. Only then could the dead make it to the Elysian Fields where they'd drink from the Lethe— the river of forgetting—and begin again as "flesh." In other words, he, too, believed in reincarnation.

I liked Aeneas. Mostly because his dad was *not* Zeus.

THE MYSTERIOUS MYSTERIES

THE ANCIENTS EVENTUALLY believed that there was yet another section of Elysium—one reserved for those who had undergone the rites of various cults called "mystery religions." Only special people could go there—those who had undergone secret rites.

No one knows exactly what these rites were. I do, of course, but if I told you, I'd have to kill you. I am not kidding. This is what my people believed. There were actual murder contracts put out on people who were suspected of giving up secrets of their "mystery" religion. This intense secrecy explains why there are no records of what actually happened during their ceremonies, even though the practice went on for a millennium.

Out of all my people's accomplishments, being able to keep a secret turned out to be one of the most impressive. Who knew?

There were many "mystery" religions—including the mysteries of Dionysus, Orpheus, Cybele, and others—but the Eleusinian Mysteries were the first and most powerful.

However, let the record show that the biggest mystery of all is why there wasn't a mystery cult named after *me*. I mean, *hellllloooo*, am I not the god of the land of the dead? What does Dionysus—yet another son of Zeus, and the god of *wine*—have to do with my world? The disrespect is never-ending, I tell you.

OLDER THAN DIRT

The Eleusinian Mysteries began so long ago, the rites were ancient even to my own people. The only thing everyone agreed on was that the rites were always devoted to the goddess of grains and fertility, my mother-in-law Demeter, and her daughter, my wife, Persephone. It was believed that Demeter had been born in the city of Eleusis, near Athens, so a pilgrimage to the city was part of the annual ceremony.

The late-September mystery festival lasted about nine days. At the heart of the ceremony were fertility rites that represented the cycles of agriculture (birth, death, and rebirth). Rituals likely included re-enactments, sacrifices, fasting, and celebrations. There may have been open-pit grilling, too.

THE IMMORTALITY BARBECUE

Supposedly, the first initiate of the Eleusinian Mysteries was a baby—a boy named Demophon.

When Persephone and I married, not only did Demeter ice-out the world, she also refused to enter Olympus because Zeus had approved the marriage. One day she went to the city of Eleusis disguised as an old woman. The king and queen brought her into their home, and Demeter was so grateful for the hospitality that she decided to give their newborn son—Demophon—the gift of immortality.

Unfortunately for him, this involved having his tiny body roasted over a fire for many nights. After a few grillings, the queen saw what Demeter was doing and cried out in alarm. Demeter grew furious with her (my mother-in-law has anger issues, remember) and took the gift of immortality away from the boy. However, through that ritual, Demophon obtained a hero's honor, which meant he would live forever in happy Elysium.

Anyone else who went through the Eleusinian Mysteries—which didn't, presumably, require being barbecued alive like Demophon—also got to live forever in Elysium.

SECRET PASSWORDS FOR IMMORTALITY

The Dionysian mystery religion was similar in that it, too, focused on themes of fertility. (Dionysus is the god of the vine.) It also was celebrated over many days and likely included a re-enactment of a trip to my realm. But followers of this religion came up with something different.

During the rituals, you learned secret passwords and directions—poetic lines, really—to recite when you met me, to ensure that you got to live forever in Elysium. The main thing was to recite this at the Lake of Memory:

I am a son of Earth and starry Sky, I am parched with thirst and am dying; but quickly grant me cold water from the Lake of Memory to drink.

If you spoke these lines, I gave you my permission to drink and then showed you the secret road to a happily-ever-after-for-eternity in Elysium.

Easy-peasy, right?

After working so hard to get to Elysium, what could all these initiates expect? Immortality, of course. A blessed land where the sun always shone and anger and misery never showed their ugly faces. Day in and day out of rubbing elbows with other smug initiates who knew the "pass code."

Sounds like hell to me. Just saying.

TIME FOR YOU TO GET
THE HECK OUT OF HADES

Well, my little mortal friend, that completes our tour of my kingdom. Good thing, too, because I am tired of showing you around. As king of the underworld, I have more important things to do.

Like what, you ask?

Well, like coming up with new punishments for evil-doers in the dungeons of Tartaros, for one. And also scouring every inch of this place to make sure that no sons of Zeus—or Poseidon, for that matter (I'm looking at you, Percy Jackson)—sneak into my realm to create yet more havoc.

In other words, it's time for you to get on out of here, young mortal. Since we're in Elysium, you can work your way backward through my realm—through Tartaros, the Grove of Persephone, past Cerberus (yeah, good luck with that), and the Styx—and then climb your way out into your world.

However, if you don't feel up to trying to convince Cerberus that he really, really doesn't need to gnaw your head off, you have another option.

In *The Aeneid*, Aeneas's dad tells him that he can *float* his way out of Elysium through either one of the Two Gates of Sleep. The only downside of dreaming your way out, though, is that some of the Oneiroi—the batlike bringers of melas oneiros or bad dreams—will likely come with you. They may then decide to roost in your room, hanging upside-down over your bed and watching you with their red eyes, waiting for you to fall asleep so they can drop their dream poop—I mean, nightmares—all over you.

So, to get out of here, you need to face either Cerberus or the Oneiroi. Up to you, kid. But make up your mind quickly. I don't have an eternity to wait for you, you know. (Oh, wait, I do. . . . Never mind.)

Whichever way you choose, I'll see you on the other side—sooner or later.

HADES'S GUIDE TO ANCIENT GREEK GODS AND HEROES

Achilles: The Greek hero of Homer's *Iliad*, the epic poem about the Trojan War. His mother was a nymph who tried to make him immortal by dipping him into the river Styx when he was an infant. She missed a spot, though, leaving the backs of his ankles vulnerable. He was eventually killed by an arrow in the heel. You moderns call that area—or any weakness, really—an "Achilles's heel." As the best warrior of all the Greeks, Achilles sent a *lot* of dead my way, so I forgave him for his surly attitude and tendency to throw tantrums.

Aeneas: The Roman hero of *The Aeneid*, written by Virgil. Aeneas was a Trojan hero who escaped the fall of Troy and, after many challenges and tribulations, founded the city of Rome. He was a son of Venus and came down to my realm to visit his father in Elysium.

Aphrodite (Venus, to the Romans): The Greek goddess of love and beauty. She was forced to marry the misshapen Hephaestus (Vulcan) but was in love with Ares (Mars), the god of war. Aphrodite once sent Psyche down here to steal my wife's beauty secrets.

Apollo: The god of music, truth, poetry, prophecy, and the sun, Apollo is the twin brother of Artemis (Diana), goddess of the hunt, and the son of Zeus and Leto. I tolerate the light-boy mainly because he has never dared to come down here to Hades, which I appreciate.

Ares (Mars): God of war, Ares isn't very smart, but he is an excellent warrior. My little brother Zeus once called him the "most hated" of all his children, but I like him a lot because, thanks to him, my realm is always crowded.

Artemis (Diana): The goddess of the hunt, Artemis is Apollo's twin sister. She protects women in childbirth, as well as young girls. She is often associated with the moon, which fits her personality—cold and distant. However, I like her because she often calls upon Hekate to wreak havoc on unruly mortals.

Athena (Minerva): Goddess of wisdom and warfare, Athena was born right out of Zeus's head, armor and all. She protected Athens and brought olives, chariots, ships, and wool-making to the Greeks. She frequently gives her father headaches, which makes me happy.

Cupid (Eros, to the Greeks): Cupid, the son of Venus, was a god of love, attraction, and affection. You moderns made him into a cherub in diapers for Valentine's Day, but he was originally a young man whose love-tipped arrows could make anyone fall in love.

Demeter (Ceres): My mother-in-law, Demeter, is the goddess of grains and the harvest. In other words, she was the original "Mother Nature." She is also quite the drama queen. Demeter has never forgiven me for marrying her daughter Persephone; she marks that occasion by causing almost everything in nature to die during the months that Persephone spends in the underworld with me.

Dionysus (Bacchus): The god of the grape harvest, winemaking, wine, and partying, Dionysus is yet another son of Zeus. He can be a bit of a wild child, but he also sent people down here with secret directions for making it to Elysium through his "mystery religion."

Hades (Pluto): Need I introduce myself again? I am the Lord of the Dead, older brother of Zeus and Poseidon. The Greeks called me "He Who Must Not Be Named." The Romans called me "Pluto," which referred to all the gold, silver, and other riches buried deep within the earth in my domain.

Hephaestus (Vulcan): The son of Zeus and Hera, Hephaestus is the god of blacksmiths, metalworking, fire, and volcanoes. He builds all kinds of cool things, such as metal automatons and magic shields. Unfortunately, he's a bit misshapen—but that didn't stop the gods from marrying him off to the goddess of love, Aphrodite (Venus).

Herakles (Hercules): The son of Zeus whom I love to hate the most, Herakles is one of the most popular and beloved of all the ancient heroes. He was known for extraordinary physical strength and courage. Amazingly, there were actual temples devoted to him (more than for me! the outrage!) and some Roman emperors even claimed they were descended from him. Plus, Roman gladiators considered him their patron godling and had shrines devoted to him. I dislike him because he came down to the underworld several times—ignoring my rules—and even stole Cerberus once!

Hermes (Mercury): Yet another son of Zeus, Hermes is the messenger god as well as the protector of travelers, thieves, and business owners. After Hermes escorted my wife down here, he became the escort for all dead people, guiding them to my realm.

Odysseus (Ulysses): The hero of Homer's *Odyssey*, Odysseus was king of Ithaca. He was known for his cunning—he was the one who came up with the Trojan horse trick that allowed the Greeks to finally defeat Troy. It took him ten years to get back to his wife, Penelope, after the Trojan War. Along the way, he had many adventures, including making a trip down here to my realm to get directions from a seer.

Orpheus: The son of Apollo and a muse named Calliope, Orpheus was the greatest musician and poet of his time. He came down to the underworld to beg for his wife back when she died soon after their wedding. I reluctantly agreed, with only one instruction—"Don't look back at your wife, Eurydice, until you are both completely out of the darkness." Unfortunately, he looked back too soon (he was out of the underworld, but she wasn't) and he lost her again.

Persephone (Proserpina): My wife and queen, Persephone embodies what happens to the earth every winter when she comes down to live with me in the underworld. When she emerges, flowers bloom and spring begins. She and her mother, Demeter, were at the center of the Eleusinian Mysteries, which promised Greeks a shot at immortality if they went through the rites.

Poseidon: My younger brother, Poseidon is the god of the oceans and is known as the "earth-shaker," the one responsible for earthquakes. Did I mention that I was born before he was?

Psyche: Originally a mortal, Psyche was a beautiful woman who fell out of sorts with Venus (it's a Roman story) and in love with Venus's son, Cupid. You can read the details of her story on page 54. She was eventually turned into a goddess when Zeus accepted her as Cupid's wife.

Theseus: Hero of Athens, this son of Poseidon is most famous for defeating the half-bull, half-human monster, the Minotaur. He came down to the underworld and accidentally left part of his backside down here! (Read what happened on page 54).

Zeus: Known as the "head Olympian" and "Father of the Gods," Zeus has control of the skies, storms, thunder, the heavens, and human justice. He claimed the juiciest portion of the world after we (emphasis on "we"!) defeated Kronos and the rest of the Titans. Have I mentioned that he was the last-born son, whereas I was the first-born? Not like it mattered to my little brother, who took the lion's share of the goods when we split the world three ways.

GLOSSARY

Aeneid, The (en-knee-id): Latin epic poem by the Roman poet Virgil; gives an account of Aeneas's founding of Rome.

ambrosia: Food of the Greek gods and demigods—sometimes in the form of a drink, other times as a food that granted immortal life.

Cocytus (koh-kie-tus): River of Lamentation in the Greek underworld.

Ekphora (ek-fo-ra): Funeral procession in ancient Greek death rites.

Eleusinian (el-ou-sin-ee-en): One of the "mystery" sects in ancient Greece that promised eternal life in Elysium.

Elysium (el-ee-see-em): Paradise-like final resting place for Greek heroes and virtuous ones.

Erinyes (air-ih-nee-yez): Three underworld goddesses who avenged murders, especially those committed against family members.

Fields of Asphodel (ass-pho-dul): A dark and gloomy no-man's land where ghosts flitted over ghostly flowers.

godlings: Demigods, usually children sired by a god or goddess and a human.

Hekatonkheries (hek-uh-tong-kuh-reez): Giant god-monsters, each of whom had one hundred hands and fifty heads. They guarded the pit of Tartaros and also released killer storms.

Herakles (Hercules): Greek hero known for his outsize strength. He was a son of Zeus and traveled down to the underworld a number of times.

Iliad, The (ill-*ee*-id): Ancient Greek epic poem written by Homer, describing the last few weeks of the Trojan War. The hero Achilles is at the center of the story.

Kronos: Titan god of time. Kronos ate his children, who would be later known as the Olympian gods.

Lamia (*lae*-mee-eye): An underworld daimon or vampire-like monster that ate children and preyed on travelers.

lemures (lem-*oor*-es): Restless ghosts or spirits of the dead.

Lemuria (lah-mure-ee-ah): Annual ancient Roman festival in which beans were tossed to the ghosts of the restless dead to keep them away from the home.

melas oneiros (mel-ess on-*air*-ohss): Nightmares; spirits of dreams that brought "black" dreams.

Moirae (*moy*-rye): Three goddesses in control of the fate of the gods and humans; sometimes called "The Fates."

Odyssey, The: Like *The Iliad*, an epic poem written by Homer. It describes Odysseus's ordeals as he tried to return home to Ithaca.

Oneiroi (on-*air*-roy): Bringers of dreams.

Phlegethon (*fleg*-ah-thon): River of Fire, one of the five rivers of the underworld.

Prothesis: Funeral rite wherein the body was cleaned, anointed, and laid out in such a way that family and friends could pay their respects.

shade: Spirit or ghost of a dead person living in the underworld.

Styx: River in the underworld that separated the underworld from the upper (or living) world.

Tartaros (*tar*-tar-us): A place below the earth in Hades; a pit within Tartaros where the spirits of the wicked were punished.

BIBLIOGRAPHY

PRIMARY SOURCES

Apuleius, *The Golden Ass*

Hesiod, *Theogeny*

Homer, *The Iliad* and *The Odyssey*

Ovid, *Metamorphoses*

Plato, *Gorgias*

Seneca, *Phaedra*

Strabo, *Geography*

Virgil, *The Aeneid*

SECONDARY SOURCES

Abel, Ernest. *Death Gods: An Encyclopedia of the Rulers, Evil Spirits and Geographies of the Dead.* Westport: Greenwood Press, 2009.

Albinus, Lars. *The House of Hades.* Netherlands: Aarhus University Press, 2000.

Cobbe, Frances Power. *Hades.* Public domain, 1864.

DiAulaire, Ingri and Edgar. *Book of Greek Myths.* New York: Doubleday, 1962.

Dova, Stamatia. *Greek Heroes in and out of Hades.* London: Lexington Books, 2012.

Feton, D. *Haunted Greece and Rome: Ghost Stories from Classical Antiquity.* Austin: University of Texas Press, 1999.

Garland, Robert. *The Greek Way of Death*. New York: Cornell University Press, 2001.

Hamilton, Edith. *Mythology: Timeless Tales of Gods and Heroes*. New York: Warner Books, 1942.

Hope, Valerie M. *Death in Ancient Rome: A Sourcebook* London: Routledge, 2007.

Matyszak, Philip. *Ancient Athens on 5 Drachmas a Day*. London: Thames & Hudson, 2008.

McKeown, J.C. *A Cabinet of Greek Curiosities*. New York: Oxford University Press, 2013.

McKeown, J.C. *A Cabinet of Roman Curiosities*. New York: Oxford University Press, 2010.

Mirto, Maria Serena. *Death in the Greek World: From Homer to the Classical Age*. Norman: University of Oklahoma Press, 2012.

Moncrieff, A.R. Hope. *Myths and Legends of Ancient Greece*. New York: Random House, 1995.

Sourvinou-Inwood, Christiane. *Reading Greek Death*. New York: Oxford University Press, 1995.

Turner, Alice K. *The History of Hell*. New York: Harcourt, 1993.

Vermeule, Emily. *Aspects of Death in Early Greek Art and Poetry*. Berkeley: University of California Press, 1979.

ARTICLES

Harrison, Jane. "Helios-Hades." *The Classical Review*. Vol. 22, No. 1 (Feb 1908).

Johnson, David M. "Hesiod's Descriptions of Tartarus." *Phoenix (Classical Association of Canada).* Spring–Summer 1999.

Miller, David L. "Hades and Dionysos: The Poetry of the Soul." *Journal of the American Academy of Religion.* XLVI.

Stephens, Wade C. "Descent to the Underworld in Ovid's Metamorphoses." *The Classical Journal.* Vol. 53, No. 4 (Jan. 1958).

WEB SOURCES

Encyclopedia Mythica: *http://www.pantheon.org/*

GreekMythology.com: *http://www.greekmythology.com/index.html*

Theoi Greek Mythology: *http://www.theoi.com/*

INDEX

WANT TO DISCOVER MORE SECRETS OF THE ANCIENT GODS? HERE'S A PEEK AT

ANUBIS SPEAKS!

A GUIDE TO THE AFTERLIFE BY THE EGYPTIAN GOD OF THE DEAD

GREETINGS, MORTAL

ALLOW ME TO INTRODUCE MYSELF. I am Anubis—the Egyptian god of the "Mysteries of Embalming," the "Guardian of the Veil of Death," "Opener of the Ways of the Dead," and if you are "bad" . . . *Your. Worst. Nightmare.*

But do not fear. I will not snatch your beating heart from your chest and toss it to my good friend, crocodile-headed Amut the Destroyer, for a squishy snack . . . not *today* anyway. Instead, I will guide you through my world of deep magic, strange gods, and gruesome monsters. I will show you how my people, the ancient Egyptians, prepared the dead for eternal life, and how we gods fought the forces of darkness and evil—every night—to keep you safe.

Oh dear, were you perhaps hoping for a less scary-looking guide to lead you through the Egyptian dark lands, one without so many razor-sharp fangs? Too bad. You're in my realm now. And I'm in charge. So pay attention.

We will, soon enough, come face-to-face with the evil one—Apophis, the snake of doom that threatens to devour and destroy the world. In my day, only our dead pharaohs—kings who turned into immortal gods upon their deaths—were strong enough to join the rest of us gods in facing the beast.

You, my little human, are no pharaoh, but I'm allowing you to come along anyway. You may thank me later, preferably in buckets of blood. Meanwhile, take heed; if you scare easily, I suggest you close this book right now and go back to coloring rainbows and unicorns.

Seriously.

There will be blood. And snakes. And decapitations. And monsters who like to gobble up hearts and squeeze heads until they pop.

Still with us?

Good. Then, please, step into my lair. . . .

THE DARK LANDS

WELCOME TO DUAT, the Egyptian afterworld. It's a little dark, yes, but what did you expect? This world only comes alive after the sun sets . . . and after you die, of course (not like I'm looking forward to that or anything).

The Egyptian Land of the Dead was sometimes called the "Twelve Hours of Darkness" for the long hours of the night. You see, my people believed that the sun was born every morning in the east at sunrise. When it disappeared in the west at sunset, they worried that evil in the dark lands would keep the sun from rising again. Without the sun, everyone and everything would die! So it became really, really important to make sure that the sun survived.

The sun's survival and rebirth also became a powerful metaphor for the individual's rebirth in the afterworld.

Lots of gods and monsters played a role in this battle between light and dark, death and eternal life. You will meet some of them on this journey. Keep in mind, there are thousands of us gods. Not only that, but the same god could appear in many different forms! So you won't get to know all of us, which is fine because really, I'm the only one that matters.

THE PEOPLE WHO
WORSHIPPED US

The ancient Egyptians first settled near the fertile banks of the Nile River around five thousand years ago. Over time they banded together to form one kingdom under the rule of pharaohs that lasted for thousands of years. (Yeah, and how long has your nation been around? Mortal, *please*. It doesn't even come close to matching our longevity!)

My people invented a type of writing called hieroglyphics. They created the first paper from papyrus. They established a calendar that became the basis for the Western calendar. And they built great pyramids, statues, and temples that continue to awe humans around the world today. In other words, while you folks in the West were just learning to walk without dragging your knuckles on the ground, my people created one of the richest and most advanced cultures of the ancient world.

You're welcome.

MAGIC AND MAYHEM

For the Egyptians, the world was a magical place where destruction and chaos could only be managed or avoided by a strict adherence to ritual, order, and worship. Praying to and honoring the gods were the glue that held Egyptian culture together. And it worked, too.

I should know.

But while we gods were the spiritual heart of the kingdom, the Nile River was its main artery.

THE GIFT OF THE NILE

The Greek writer Herodotus called Egypt "The Gift of the Nile." He was right. The Nile is like a thin thread of life in a wasteland of desert. The deserts on either side of the Nile, which Egyptians called the "red lands," provided a natural barrier from attack by invaders. The "black lands" of the Nile referred to the rich soil left on the banks after its annual flooding or inundation. Thanks to the fertility of the black lands, Egypt became known as the breadbasket of the ancient world. The Nile was also the primary means of transportation, trade, and travel.

The great river was an important symbol of my people's religion, too. It separated east from west— east, where the sun was born, and west, where it set into the dark lands. Most mummies were buried on the west side of the Nile—in the red lands—in honor of this division. Most dead pharaohs took a symbolic journey on the Nile. Their bodies were carried on a funeral barge as they traveled to their eternal tombs.

With as much as my people owed the Nile, it's no surprise that their creation stories featured life-giving waters. There are three primary Egyptian creation myths, all beginning with the dark, primeval waters of

Nun (or abyss). I will only tell you the one story that is related to *me* because, of course, it's the only one that matters.

Egyptian Creation Myth
from the City of the Sun

IN THE BEGINNING, there was nothing but an endless swirling sea of chaos known as the dark primeval waters of Nun. The god Atum-Re (also known as Atum-Ra or Ra) willed himself into existence. He wanted to stand on something so he created a hill, which the Egyptians called Iunu, and the Greeks called Heliopolis (City of the Sun).

Atum brought light to the world by becoming a Bennu bird (heron). The Bennu bird perched on the hill and let out a honk so great, it called existence into being.

But Atum was lonely, so with a mighty glob of spit and snot he created his children, Shu, the god of air, and Tefnut, the goddess of moisture and water.

Shu and Tefnut had children of their own—Geb, god of the earth, and Nut, goddess of the sky. Geb lay down on the surface of the water, creating land. Nut arced over him, shining with light during the day and twinkling with stars at night.

Nut and Geb had four children: Isis, Osiris, Set, and Nephthys. The Egyptians called all of these gods, including Atum-Re, the Pesdjet, the Nine, or in Greek, the Ennead of Heliopolis—the first gods of Egypt.

How is this story related to me? Two of these first gods, Osiris and Nephthys, are my parents. That alone makes them worthy of special worship, don't you think?

UNDERSTANDING RA (SOMETIMES CALLED ATUM), THE GOD WHO CREATED THE WORLD BY HOCKING A GIANT LOOGIE

Protecting Ra from the monster Apophis is why we are here, folks. And yes, I agree that it's a little undignified to know we all came from what Ra spit up when he was bored. But still, we owe him, right?

My people told many stories about Ra, the creator god, but the following one is my favorite because it features so much human death and destruction. And blood. Lots and lots of human blood (*mmmm*, my favorite snack). Plus it explains why Ra left us so he could travel alone across the sky as the sun, or what we called the sun disk.

And why, you may ask, did Ra refuse to continue walking among his creations on earth? Because you humans had to go and ruin it for the rest of us. You plotted against him. You rebelled, thinking to steal Ra's power (as if) for yourself.

Ra withdrew into the sky in response to your sacrilege. So it's all your fault, you petty, backstabbing, power-hungry, smelly little mortals.

But I'm not resentful.

Really, I'm not.

Ra's Bloody Revenge

RA RULED ALL THAT HE CREATED, including gods and humans. But Ra grew old and tired. His bones became silver, his flesh gold, and his hair lapis lazuli. Some humans thought he was too old to rule. They wanted his power and plotted against him.

Furious, Ra called a secret meeting of the gods. "How should I punish those who plot to overthrow me?" the great god thundered.

Nun of the watery abyss advised him to get rid of the rebels. For good.

So Ra sent the goddess Hathor after them. She normally presented herself as a kindly, milk-giving cow. But Hathor also had a vengeful angry side known as Sekhmet, the lion-headed goddess.

Sekhmet pounced on the human evildoers who had fled to the desert. With a mighty roar, she devoured them and lapped up their blood before it could sink into the desert sands. Sekhmet discovered she relished the taste of human blood. She wanted more . . . and more.

She began to stalk good people, too; those who honored Ra and would never have plotted against him. But Ra was not a vengeful god. He did not want all of humankind destroyed. He called Sekhmet back. But with the blood matting the fur on her face, she only roared,

"Mmmmm, good. More! Must have more human blood!" And off she went on the hunt again. She vowed to keep hunting until all of humanity was destroyed.

Ra had to do something to stop her, so he came up with a plan. He sent his fastest messengers to gather the reddest clay they could find, bright red dirt called ochre. He ordered his servants to brew seven thousand clay jars of beer, and then he had the red ochre mixed in with the drink. As Sekhmet slept, Ra's servants emptied all seven thousand jars of beer into a field before her. She awoke to what seemed like a lake of blood and pounced on it, gulping it down.

But soon she grew full and woozy. After one mighty belch, she lay down to sleep. When she awoke she saw the remnants of the "blood" lake and thought, "My work here is done. I have killed all the humans in the world."

Her rage gone, Sekhmet turned back into Hathor, the placid divine cow, and returned to Ra. Ra was happy to have Hathor back, but he continued to resent humans for plotting against him. After all, if they had done so once, they would likely do so again.

"I am old and tired," Ra announced. "I wish to sink back into the waters of Nun until I am ready to be born again." He wanted to undo all that he had created!

So Nun called upon the sky goddess Nut to help Ra. Nut transformed into a cow with golden flanks and gilded horns, and told Ra to climb on her back. He did so and she carried him high into the heavens. But Nut grew dizzy at the height of the sun, and Ra called upon many gods, including Shu, the god of air, to support her as she supported him.

Removing himself to the heavens during the day meant Ra also traveled to the underworld at night to do battle with Apophis, the spirit of darkness and chaos. The people of earth, however, were frightened by the darkness and called out to Ra.

"I will provide light until I am born again," Ra announced. "I appoint Thoth as my assistant on earth." Ra commanded Thoth to provide some light during the dark hours. Thoth, then, came to represent the moon, as well as wisdom.

Ra always returned at dawn with the sunrise, though he never again mixed with the people and world he created.

Remember, young mortal, it was you humans and your greedy grasping that led to Ra's departure. So keep it under control while you're with me, or else. . . .